HARRIS COUNTY PUBLIC LIBRARY

Galaxies

HOWARD K. TRAMMEL

Children's Press®
A Division of Scholastic Inc.
New York Toronto London Auckland Sydney
Mexico City New Delhi Hong Kong
Danbury, Connecticut

Content Consultant
Noreen Grice
Astronomer
President, You Can Do Astronomy, LLC.
www.youcandoastronomy.com

Library of Congress Cataloging-in-Publication Data

Trammel, Howard K., 1957-
    Galaxies / by Howard K. Trammel.
        p. cm.—(A true book)
    Includes index.
    ISBN-13: 978-0-531-16896-7 (lib. bdg.)   978-0-531-22803-6 (pbk.)
    ISBN-10: 0-531-16896-4 (lib.bdg)   0-531-22803-7 (pbk.)

1. Galaxies—Juvenile literature. 2. Milky Way—Juvenile literature. I. Title. II. Series.

QB857.3.T73 2010
523.1'12—dc22   2008051268

1 2 3 4 5 6 7 8 9 10 R 19 18 17 16 15 14 13 12 11 10   62

Find the Truth!

Everything you are about to read is true *except* for one of the sentences on this page.

Which one is **TRUE**?

T or F　Galaxies can collide with each other.

T or F　The Milky Way is the biggest galaxy.

Find the answers in this book.

The Armagh Observatory in Northern Ireland

Contents

THE BIG TRUTH!

A Closer Look

Andromeda galaxy

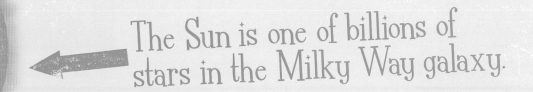

The Sun is one of billions of stars in the Milky Way galaxy.

Hubble Space Telescope

The Milky Way

CHAPTER 1

What Is a Galaxy?

A **galaxy** (GAL-uhk-see) is a giant collection of gas, dust, and stars. All the stars you can see in the clear night sky are part of our galaxy, which is called the **Milky Way**. Scientists think that in addition to the Milky Way, there are billions of other galaxies.

The Chinese called the Milky Way the Silver River.

The Milky Way is just one of many galaxies in the **universe** (YOO-nuh-vurss). The universe is huge and includes space and galaxies. On a clear night, away from bright city lights, you can see a band of light across the sky. This is the Milky Way galaxy.

People had wondered what the Milky Way was for thousands of years. They couldn't tell that it was made of billions of stars. The Romans called it the Milky Way because it reminded them of milk.

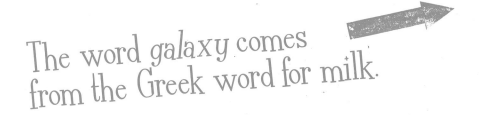

The word *galaxy* comes from the Greek word for milk.

The Greeks' early observations of space helped lead the way to more discoveries.

Prolemeus

Aftonomia

CHAPTER 2

All About the Milky Way

The Milky Way is shaped like a giant disk with a bar of stars in the middle. The middle is where the stars are most crowded together. The Milky Way has curved arms that spin out from its center. The arms wrap around the center, forming a spiral shape. Our **solar system** (SOH-lur SISS-tuhm), which includes Earth and the Sun, is near one of the arms of the Milky Way.

The Milky Way's arms are named after constellations.

Even though the stars of the Milky Way are our neighbors in space, they are actually very far away. Scientists had to create a special way to measure this distance. It's called a light-year. A light-year measures how far light travels in one Earth year or 365 1/4 days. A light-year is about 5.9 trillion miles (about 10 trillion kilometers). Our closest star neighbor in the Milky Way is more than four light-years away.

Promixa Centauri is our closest star neighbor. The Latin word for "close" is Proxima.

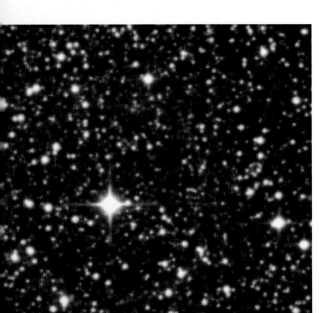

The brightest star toward the center of this image is Proxima Centauri.

This is what the Milky Way might look like if we could see it from the side.

Spiral Arm

Center

The center of the Milky Way is full of mostly old stars. Its spiral arms contain more newborn stars.

The Milky Way is huge! Scientists think that it contains up to 400 billion stars. Earth is about 30,000 light-years from the center of the Milky Way. It would take 100,000 years to travel from one edge of the Milky Way to the other.

Spinning Through Time

Scientists believe that the Milky Way is one of the older galaxies in the universe. It was formed about 13.6 billion years ago and has been spinning in space ever since. Our solar system spins with it, circling the center of the galaxy. It takes our solar system about 225 million years to make one complete **orbit** (OR-bit) of the Milky Way. Since the Sun and our solar system are about 4.6 billion years old, we have orbited the galaxy less than 20 times since our solar system was born.

The Milky Way

Our Solar System

Our solar system is only a tiny part of the Milky Way.

14

Charles Messier and Messier Objects

Charles Messier was a French **astronomer** (uh-STRON-uh-mur) in the 1700s. He made a list of the bright objects he saw in the sky. Even though he didn't know it at the time, many of those objects were actually galaxies. Today, we still call these objects Messier Objects. With a simple **telescope** (TEL-uh-skope), you can view Messier Objects, too.

The Triangulum galaxy (shown here) is number 33 on Messier's list. It's called M33.

The Milky Way's Neighborhood

The Milky Way is not alone in our part of the universe. Scientists call the Milky Way, and the galaxies nearby, the Local Group. There are dozens of galaxies in the Local Group. One of them is the Andromeda galaxy. It is the same size as the Milky Way, and is one of our closest neighbors. The Andromeda galaxy is about 2.5 million light-years away from Earth.

There are two galaxies that are much closer to the Milky Way than the Andromeda galaxy. They are called the Large Magellanic Cloud and the Small Magellanic Cloud.

A view of the Milky Way from the Southern Hemisphere

Small Magellanic Cloud

Large Magellanic Cloud

The Large Magellanic Cloud

The Magellanic Clouds are named after Ferdinand Magellan, the first sailor to travel all the way around Earth.

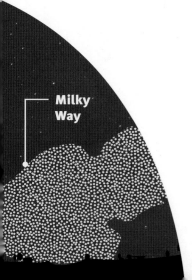

Milky Way

The Large Magellanic Cloud is about 170,000 light-years away from the Milky Way. The Small Magellanic Cloud is 200,000 light-years away. Below the equator, in the Southern Hemisphere, these galaxies can be seen in the sky. They look like puffs of clouds among the stars.

The Sombrero galaxy got its name because it looks like a Mexican hat.

CHAPTER 3

Galaxies Galore

Beside stars, galaxies are also filled with gas and dust. Galaxies with lots of gas and dust usually have more stars. The new stars are made of gas and dust. In some galaxies, there is not as much gas and dust. These materials have already been used up to make existing stars.

The Sombrero galaxy was discovered in 1781.

Types of Galaxies

All galaxies are not alike. They have different numbers of stars and different shapes. But most galaxies fit into one of three main groups. These groups are spiral galaxies, elliptical galaxies, and irregular galaxies.

Spiral galaxies have older stars at their centers, and lots of gas and dust in their spiral arms. The arms are where new stars are still forming.

The Whirlpool galaxy is a spiral galaxy.

20

Elliptical galaxy

Spiral galaxies sometimes form a bar of stars across their middle. These are called barred spiral galaxies. The Milky Way is a barred spiral galaxy.

Elliptical galaxies are usually shaped like either a circle or an oval. Their shape is not as easy to recognize as that of a spiral galaxy. The stars in an elliptical galaxy tend to be older. These galaxies may have used up a lot of the gas and dust inside them to make stars.

The irregular galaxy NGC 1569 creates stars 100 times faster than the Milky Way does.

Irregular galaxies aren't spiral or elliptical and can be spread out in any shape. They are usually made up of a lot of gas and dust. Often they have many young stars, and they are still making more stars. There is only one irregular galaxy on Messier's list. It's called M82, the Cigar galaxy.

Cigar galaxy

Groups and Clusters

Just as the Milky Way is part of the Local Group, other galaxies are also found in groups. Collections of less than 50 galaxies are called groups. When there are more than 50 galaxies together, they are called clusters. Clusters have hundreds of galaxies in them. Both clusters of galaxies and groups of galaxies can be found near each other. Scientists call these groupings **superclusters** (SOO-pur-kluhss-turs).

The Virgo Cluster contains many hundreds of galaxies.

23

Space Smash

Sometimes galaxies in the same group collide or crash into one another. When galaxies collide, it's different from if you bumped into another person on the sidewalk. The stars in galaxies are far apart, so two galaxies can pass right through each other without their stars ever touching. Scientists believe that billions of years from now, the Milky Way and the Andromeda galaxy could run into each other.

Sagittarius Dwarf Galaxy

Scientists believe that a small galaxy called the Sagittarius Dwarf Galaxy is now becoming a part of the Milky Way.

Millions of stars are formed as the Antennae galaxies collide.

When galaxies collide, different things can happen. Sometimes a larger galaxy will absorb a smaller galaxy. When two spiral galaxies collide, their arms change shape and become twisted. At times, one galaxy will take the gas and dust from another galaxy. When the gas and dust of a galaxy are moved around by another galaxy, it often leads to the creation of new stars.

Space Telescopes

The Hubble Space Telescope orbits outside of Earth's atmosphere (AT-muhss-fihr). Even though air looks clear to us, if you try to look through miles of moving air things look fuzzy. Orbiting outside of Earth's atmosphere, where there is no air, allows the Hubble to take extremely clear pictures.

Refracting Telescopes

The first telescopes were refracting (ree-FRAK-ting) telescopes. They use two simple lenses like magnifying glasses to see things that are farther away. The main lens is used to gather light. It works like a funnel, taking a wide view of light and directing it through the eyepiece as a smaller picture.

Eyepiece

Lens

Light enters telescope

Reflecting Telescopes

Reflecting telescopes use a primary mirror to gather light. Then another mirror reflects the light into the eyepiece.

Light enters telescope

Eyepiece

Mirrors

A Closer Look

For many centuries, scientists could only look up at the sky with their eyes. It was impossible for them to see that the Milky Way was made of stars, or that the Magellanic Clouds were galaxies. But when the telescope was invented, sky watchers were able to see farther than ever before.

The Hubble is a really big reflecting telescope.

The Aztecs lived in Mexico for hundreds of years. Their calendar, like the one shown below, had pictures for days, months, and cycles of the Sun.

CHAPTER 4

The First Science

Astronomy (uh-STRON-uh-mee) is called the first science, because people have always studied the stars in the sky. Early sky watchers discovered that there were patterns to how the stars moved. They learned to keep track of the passing months and years according to these movements. Ancient people in the Middle East and South America made calendars based on patterns they observed in the Sun, Moon, and stars.

The Aztecs carved their calendar into stone.

Over the Moon

About the year 1608, people learned to put two lenses together in a tube to make the first telescopes. An astronomer named Galileo (gal-ih-LAY-o) used the new invention to explore space. He looked at the Moon and then at other planets and the Milky Way. Galileo was the first person to state that the Milky Way was made up of many stars.

Galileo

With his telescope, Galileo discovered four moons orbiting Jupiter. These were the first moons found around another planet.

Spotting Stars

In the 1700s, an astronomer named William Herschel wanted to learn about the shape of our galaxy. He used his telescope to count the stars, and came up with an idea based on this

In 1789, William Herschel built a telescope that was 40 feet (12 meters) long. It was the largest telescope in the world for many years.

information. Where there were more stars, he thought the galaxy would be thicker. Based on his idea, Herschel thought that the Milky Way was shaped like a flattened disk. He thought our Sun was at the center of the Milky Way. People believed this for a long time.

The Andromeda galaxy is one of the farthest space objects that you can see without a telescope.

With the help of telescopes, astronomers could see that the Andromeda galaxy and the Magellanic Clouds were made up of stars. There were actually many clouds of stars like these in the night sky. But astronomers didn't know they were galaxies. Most scientists thought that these clouds of stars were much smaller and closer to Earth than they really were. Up to 100 years ago, they thought the Milky Way was the whole universe.

Reaching for the Stars

In the 1920s, astronomer Edwin Hubble came up with a new way to measure the distance to other galaxies. He figured out that a star's brightness helped tell how close or far away it was from Earth. Just as if you walk away from a light, it seems less bright, the farther we were from a star, the less bright it would appear.

By measuring how bright the star seemed to be, Hubble could tell how far away it was. He proved that galaxies like the Andromeda galaxy were outside the Milky Way. This confirmed that the universe is millions of times bigger than our galaxy.

Edwin Hubble

This picture shows many distant galaxies in the galaxy cluster called Abell 1689.

Growing Universe

When Edwin Hubble proved that the universe was much bigger than the Milky Way, he noticed something else. Distant galaxies all seemed to be racing away from us! In every direction, the farthest galaxies were getting farther away. Scientists wondered why galaxies didn't come to the end of the universe and have to stop. Edwin Hubble and other scientists figured out that it was because the universe was getting bigger all the time.

The Big Bang Theory

Scientists think that if the universe is expanding now, it must have been smaller in the past. They believe the universe started out squeezed into one small space, and then began expanding. This idea is called the Big Bang Theory. If you drew dots on a balloon, and started blowing it up, the dots would all move further away from each other as the balloon filled with air.

The universe is expanding like that balloon, and the galaxies are the dots, all moving away from each other.

The Palomar Observatory in California
has a 200 inch (5 m) telescope.

CHAPTER 5

Looking Farther

Using telescopes, astronomers have looked far out into space and learned a lot about the Milky Way and many other galaxies. But they always want to see even farther, so they have designed bigger telescopes to help them do this. Some of these telescopes fill entire buildings called **observatories** (uhb-ZUR-vuh-tor-ees).

The Palomar Dome is 135 ft. (41 m) high and 137 ft. (41.76 m) across.

A Telescope in Space

Even with the biggest and strongest telescopes, it's challenging for astronomers to see far into space. The Earth's atmosphere always gets in the way. Scientists realized that the best place for a telescope was in orbit around Earth. With a telescope outside of Earth's atmosphere, they would be able to see farther than ever before.

In 1990, NASA launched the Hubble Space Telescope. The Hubble is like a combination of a robotic spacecraft and a telescope. It's shaped like a telescope and orbits around Earth every 97 minutes, traveling at almost 5 mi. (8 km) per second. Hubble gets its power from two huge solar panels that turn sunlight into electricity. The main mirror for the telescope is almost 8 ft. (2.4 m) across. The Hubble has no crew on board, but astronauts travel into space to make sure it's working properly.

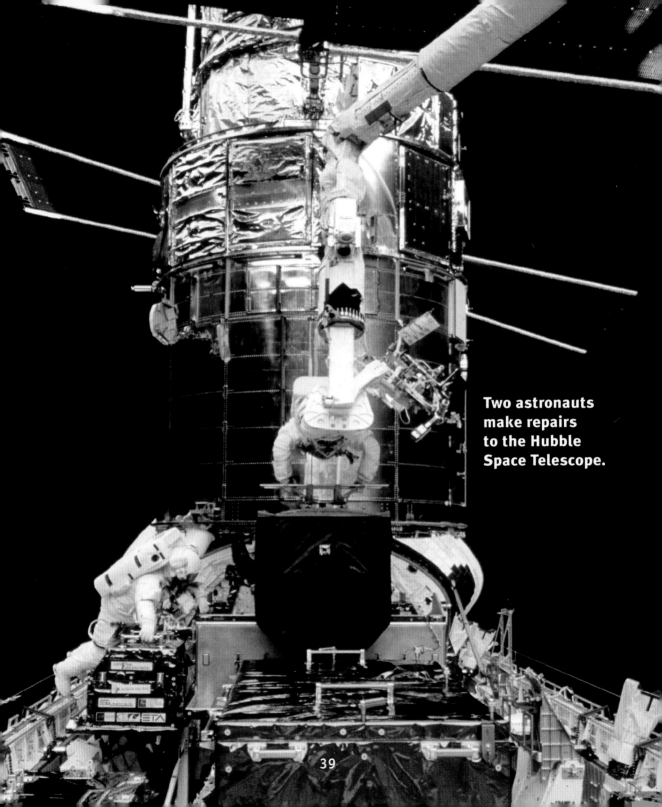

Two astronauts make repairs to the Hubble Space Telescope.

Tail

The Hubble Space Telescope took this image of two galaxies that are moving toward each other. They are nicknamed "The Mice" because they have long tails of stars and gas.

The Hubble Space Telescope, named after Edwin Hubble, has taken pictures of more than 14,000 different objects in space. It has seen farther and taken clearer pictures than any other telescope. The Hubble has helped scientists learn what galaxies looked like long ago, when the universe was young.

Key Discoveries About Galaxies

1520
The explorer Magellan observes the Magellanic Clouds.

1610
Galileo concludes the Milky Way is made up of stars.

The early universe had a greater number of small galaxies than there are now. Some scientists think that the smaller galaxies were blobby and irregular. They believe that those small, early galaxies came together to form the spiral and elliptical galaxies we see today.

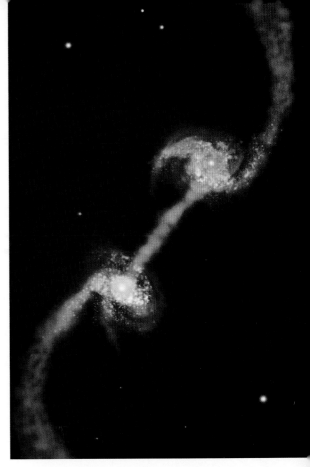

This illustration shows two galaxies about to collide.

1774

Charles Messier publishes his first list of Messier Objects.

Galaxy Messier 81

1929

Edwin Hubble demonstrates that the universe is expanding.

Future Discoveries

With the Hubble and other space telescopes, astronomers can see farther into space than ever before. The Hubble Space Telescope has sent back many amazing pictures of distant galaxies from which astronomers will continue to learn new information. And scientists are already working on new telescopes that will help them see even farther and better so they can discover still more about galaxies. ★

NASA's newest telescope is the Fermi Gamma Ray Space Telescope.

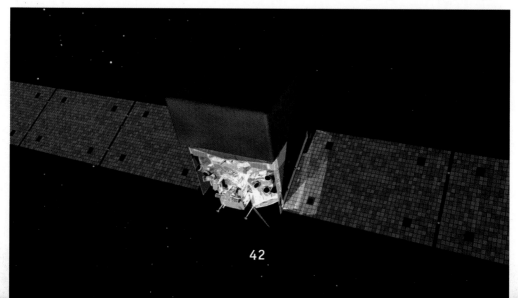

True Statistics

Number of stars in the Milky Way:
Up to 400 billion

Distance of the farthest galaxy from Earth:
About 13 billion light-years away

Number of stars that can be seen without a telescope: Thousands

Number of stars in a small galaxy:
Less than one billion

Year that Galileo first used a telescope: 1608

Weight of the Hubble Space Telescope:
24,500 pounds (11,113 kilograms)

Did you find the truth?

(T) Galaxies can collide with each other.

(F) The Milky Way is the biggest galaxy.

Resources

Books

Aguilar, David A. *Planets, Stars, and Galaxies: A Visual Encyclopedia of Our Universe.* Washington, D.C.: National Geographic, 2007.

Davis, Kenneth C. *Don't Know Much About Space.* New York: HarperCollins, 2001.

Jackson, Ellen, and Nic Bishop. *The Mysterious Universe: Supernovae, Dark Energy, and Black Holes.* Boston: Houghton Mifflin, 2008.

Mitton, Jacqueline, and Simon Mitton. *Scholastic Encyclopedia of Space.* New York: Scholastic, Inc., 1999.

Simon, Seymour. *Destination, Space.* New York: Smithsonian/Collins, 2006.

Wright, Kenneth. *Scholastic Atlas of Space.* New York: Scholastic Reference, 2004.

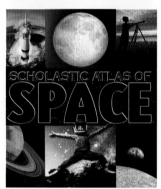

Organizations and Web Sites

Hubble Space Telescope

www.nasa.gov/mission_pages/hubble/main/index.html
Learn more about the Hubble and see lots of great pictures taken by it.

The European South Observatory

www.eso.org/gallery/v/ESOPIA/Galaxies
View pictures from one of the biggest telescopes on Earth.

Cool Cosmos

http://coolcosmos.ipac.caltech.edu/
Check out this site about astronomy that is just for kids.

Places to Visit

The Hayden Planetarium

Central Park West at 79th St.
New York, NY 10024
(212) 769 5910
www.haydenplanetarium.org/
Take a 3-D tour of the universe.

Smithsonian National Air and Space Museum

National Mall Building
Independence Avenue
at 6th St., SW
Washington, D.C. 20560
(202) 633 1000
www.nasm.si.edu/
See a huge collection of spacecraft and other space objects.

Important Words

astronomer (uh-STRON-uh-mur) – a scientist who specializes in the study of space

astronomy (uh-STRON-uh-mee) – the study of space and things we find in space

atmosphere (AT-muhss-fihr) – the layer of gases that surround a planet

galaxy (GAL-uhk-see) – a large group of stars, dust, and gas gathered together in space

Milky Way – the galaxy that includes Earth and our solar system

observatories (uhb-ZUR-vuh-tor-ees) – buildings used for observing the sky with a telescope

orbit (OR-bit) – the path around a planet or star

solar system (SOH-lur SISS-tuhm) – a star and all of the objects that travel around it

superclusters (SOO-pur-kluhss-turs) – groups of clusters of galaxies

telescope (TEL-uh-skope) – a tool for seeing farther than is possible with the naked eye

universe (YOO-nuh-vurss) – Earth, the planets, the stars, and all the things that exist in space

Index

Page numbers in **bold** indicate illustrations

About the Author

Howard K. Trammel writes fiction and nonfiction books for adults and children. He lives in New York City, where it's hard to see the stars at night. Whenever he can, he goes out in the country and looks up at the night sky.